Computer for Begi

Computer for Beginners

Zico Pratama Putra

Kanzul Ilmi Press

2018

First Printing: 2018

ISBN-13: 978-1722095611

ISBN-10: 172209561X

Kanzul Ilmi Press
Woodside Ave.
London, UK

Bookstores and wholesalers: Please contact Kanzul Ilmi Press email

zico.pratama@gmail.com.

Trademark Acknowledgments

Ordering Information: Special discounts are available on quantity purchases by corporations, associations, educators, and others. For details, contact the publisher at the above-listed address.

INTRODUCTION

This book contains courses' lessons on:

- computer introduction,
- Microsoft Windows,
- computer networks,
- computer dangers and security.

It does not contain the parts on Microsoft Word, Microsoft Excel, financial functions, Microsoft Access, computer algorithms, SPSS, Visual Basic for Applications, which are very well covered by the respective courses' suggested books.

This book is usually updated every year; please take a look at the edition date.

Disclaimers

This book is designed for very novice computer users. It often contains oversimplifications of reality, and every technical detail is purposely omitted. Expert users will find this book useless and, for certain aspects, partially wrong.

This book supposes that the user is using Microsoft Windows 7 operating system in English language. However, most of the book is perfectly readable with other Windows versions, while some menus and instructions can be rather different if the language is not English (Windows language may be changed on multi-language installations: see page 7 for further information).

The novice user in this book is, for simplicity, always considered male. This is not meant to be gender discrimination.

CONTENTS

1. COMPUTERS

This chapter presents with a brief description of computer main components, of the most common devices and of the typical software components for novice user.

1.1. Storage

1.1.1. Measures

Before starting with the computer description, it is useful to become proficient with the data size terminology, which will often be used in this book.

Computers have a very elementary way to store data: they can remember only 0 or 1. A value of 0 or 1 is called bit and all computer data are stored as sequences of bits. A sequence of 8 bits is called a byte, which is a quantity large enough to store usually a letter or a digit (even though sometimes 2 bytes are necessary). Modern computers are able to deal with enormous quantity of bytes, forcing us to introduce other quantities:

- Kilobyte (KB), approximately 1,000 bytes,
- Megabyte (MB), approximately 1,000 KB or one million bytes,
- Gigabyte (GB), approximately 1,000 MB or one billion bytes,
- Terabyte (TB), approximately 1,000 GB or one trillion bytes.

Usually, the unformatted text of a whole book can fit in some KB, while for an image in a good resolution (let's say ready to be printed on A4 paper) or for a modern song some MB are required, while a film in high quality needs some GB.

1.1.2. Moore's law

Over the last 40 years, computer hardware has been continuously improving its performances with an exponential growth. This growth is summarized by the famous Moore's law which says that the number of transistors in a processor doubles every 18 months. This law can be extended to almost every aspect of hardware, and we may say that the performance (be it speed or capacity) of hardware doubles every 18 months, thus leading to a general exponential growth. Unfortunately, software's performance does not increase with the same rate.

1.1.3. Devices

The computer uses several devices to permanently store and move data, which vary a lot in terms of capability, cost, speed, and portability.

The most used is the internal hard disk, which usually is inside the computer box and can not be moved. Its size currently ranges from 500 GB to 2 TB. On the other hand, an external hard disk is outside the computer, has the same size and obviously can be moved. Its only disadvantage is being slightly slower.

SSD Solid State Drives are starting to slowly invade the market. They are not disks at all, but very large memory cards shaped like a hard disks which can entirely replace the internal hard disk. Their main advantages are that not having moving parts (they do not rotate at high speed like hard disks) are more robust and that in most situations they are faster than hard disks (up to 10 times faster). Their disadvantage is the limited size which currently is 500 GB and their high price.

 CD and DVD in an alternative way to store data. They contain about 700 MB and 4 GB, respectively. They are divided into R which may only be written once, and RW which may be written are re-written several times. They require a CD-reader or a DVD-reader to be read, which are available on most computers, and a CD-writer or DVD-writer to be written, which are available only on some computers. A new generation of high capacity discs has appeared on the market, the Blu-ray with 25 GB size.

 Memory stick or USB pen drive is the most used way to temporary store and move data. Its size is now up to 64 GB. However its reliability is not perfect, therefore it is used mostly to move data.

Other common ways to store and move data are through a memory card, used by external devices such as photo cameras, mobile phones or music players.

1.2. Software

Software can be divided into three big categories: operating systems, programs and data.

The operating system takes care of controlling computer hardware and human-computer interaction. There are currently three widely used operating systems:

 Microsoft Windows, which is the market leader,

 Macintosh computers have their own operating system, Mac OS X,

 Linux (it is a family of very similar operating systems), which is a costless operating system,

 Android, a family of very similar Linux-based operating systems for mobile devices,

 iOS, for Apple mobile devices,

 Windows Phone, Microsoft's operating system for mobile devices.

Programs are software which is used to do particular tasks, e.g., Word for document writing, Explorer for Internet navigation, the Calculator for mathematical operations.

Data is everything which is produced either by the user or by programs (sometimes even by the operating system) to store information, e.g., a document file produced by Word is data, a downloaded web page is data.

1.2.1. Software licenses

Software can be divided, from a commercial point of view, using two features: the cost and the permission to be modified.

Subdivision by cost is:

- freeware, software which is completely costless. The producers of this software are either public institutions such as universities, or developers who do it for personal interest or advertisement or private company who do it for dumping reasons. Some examples are Skype communication program or Linux operating system;

- shareware, software which is initially cost less but after a certain period the user is asked to pay a fee or delete it; or software which has two versions: a free one, but incomplete or with advertisement banners, and a complete advertisement-free one, for which the user must pay. The most popular examples are mobile phones apps;
- commercial, software for which the user has to pay a license to use it. Common examples are Microsoft Windows operating system or Photoshop image editing program;
- subscription-based, software for which the user pays a periodic fee to use it. This software typically is also offered on the web and in this case the user does not have to care about installation nor updates. Example are Microsoft Office 365 and Photoshop Creative Clouds;
- private, software uniquely built, underpayment, for a specific customer to fit his needs. Only the customer may use it. A typical example is the university's students-courses-exams-professors database system.

The permission to be modified can seem a trivial question for the novice user, however for program developers and computer experts being authorized to modify a software is a great advantage since it can be improved, checked for errors and tailored to specific needs. The "open source versus proprietary software" is a strong ethical and economical debate in the computer scientists' community. Subdivision by permission to modify is:

- open source software may be studied, used and especially modified by anyone. The software developers at the same time legally authorize any modification, and they distribute the source of the software to put other developers in a condition to easily modify it. Open source software is also automatically freeware. The most typical example is Linux operating system.
- copyleft software is open source but carries the restriction that any modification must be distributed as open source and copyleft, thus impeding that software becomes, after a modification, proprietary. The most famous copyleft contract license is the GNU Public License (see http://www.gnu.org/licenses/gpl.html).
- proprietary software is distributed (costless as Adobe Acrobat Reader, or as a shareware as WinZip, or most often sold as commercial software as Microsoft Office) with the explicit legal warning not to modify it and technically locked to prevent other developers to see or modify its source.

1.2.2. Software naming

Software is usually identified by a name, for example "Linux" or "Microsoft Office", sometimes by a distribution/edition name "Linux Ubuntu", "Microsoft Office Professional" and very often by a version number, a sequence of numbers, points and letters (sometimes, as for Windows, commercial names) which distinguishes the changes made by developers with time, such as "Linux Ubuntu 13.10" or "Microsoft Office Professional 2013". Obviously, the version numbers of open source software changes rapidly, due to the many developers working on them.

1.2.3. Data format licenses

Data need to be saved with a certain structure, called formats. For example, a plain text file may be simply saved as a sequence of letters and symbols, which corresponds to the TXT format. More complex structures, such as images, videos, but also formatted texts, need more elaborated formats to be stored. These formats may be:

- closed proprietary, a format owned by a software company and kept as a trade secret. In this way only programs build by that company can use those data files and no other company is able to endanger its monopoly. A famous example is DOC format which, until 2007, was kept secret by Microsoft, thus preventing competitors from building alternatives to Microsoft Word program.

- open proprietary, a format publicly available but whose improvements and control are under the ownership of a software company. A typical example is the new Word format DOCX.
- open, a publicly available format which follows official standards whose control is under ownership of public organizations, such as American ANSI, German DIN or Italian UNI. Typical examples are image's format GIF or formatted text's format PDF or web page's format HTML.

2.MICROSOFT WINDOWS

Microsoft Windows is currently the market leader operating system; it is the usual interface which appears when the user turns on a personal computer with Windows operating system.

2.1.Versions and editions

Microsoft released Windows XP in 2001, and for many years it has been the main Microsoft operative system. In June 2014 it is still installed on approximately 5% of computers (source www.w3schools.com, November 2014).

Windows Vista was released in 2007, and it was not a market success. Currently, it is installed on less than 1% of computers.

Microsoft released Windows 7 in 2009, which is the currently more widespread Microsoft operative system. It is installed on approximately 57% of computers. Its editions are:

- Starter and Home Basic, cheap versions with severe limitations, used mostly on small notebooks;
- Home Premium, home user's edition;
- Professional, personal business' edition which includes more network programs;
- Enterprise/Ultimate, Professional edition with more network utilities available to companies/individual users. Enterprise edition is currently (December 2014) installed on some UNIBZ computers.

Microsoft released Windows 8 in 2013 with a new user interface called and designed for tablets with touch screen, which was not welcomed by many professional users, in order to increase compatibility with its mobile device's operating system Windows Phone 8. With its first update, Microsoft decided to change name to Windows 8.1. It is installed on approximately 21% of computers. It is available in only three editions. Enterprise edition is currently (December 2014) installed on most UNIBZ computers.

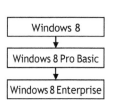

On some computers, a multi-boot system is installed. When the computer is switched on, it asks the user which operating system he would like to use and, after a short time, it starts with the default operating system. In case the user wants to use a different operating systems, he obviously must restart the computer.

2.1.1. Computer locking problem

Microsoft Windows sometimes becomes unstable: it can unpredictably, without any warning and when the user does not expect it and typically when he is doing something very important and urgent, lock and refuse to respond to user's actions. When this happens, it is usually caused by the program that is used and therefore the first thing to do is to try to close the current program. If this does not improve the situation, the only other solution left is to turn off the computer. The list of operations to try until the computer answers to user's commands is:

1. if the mouse works, click the X button on the program window or otherwise press ALT+F4;
2. press CTRL+SHIFT+ESC; select the program from the list and press End Program;
3. press CTRL+ALT+DEL and, from the bottom right icon, choose Shut Down;
4. press the computer on/off button;
5. unplug the electric power.

In any case, all the current unsaved work will be lost; in the last two cases the operating system can sometimes be damaged, but very often it will repair by itself the next time the computer is turned on. Therefore it is always a very good idea to save very often the current work, especially when it is important, urgent, or difficult to redo.

2.2. Regional and language settings

With a multilanguage Windows installation, keyboard settings or menus' languages may be changed pressing Windows+I and then choosing on the sidebar "Control panel." Then, as soon as the Control Panel opens up, click on "Clock, Language and Region", then "Language". Here, there is the possibility for the computer's administrator to download additional language's packages and then to modify the language used by Windows.

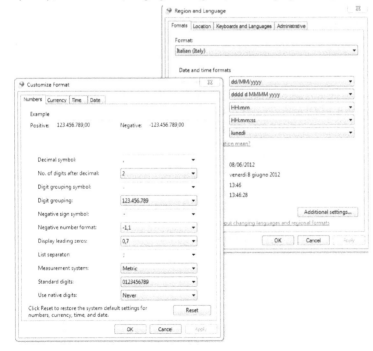

Another interesting option, available on every Windows installation, is the numbers' and dates' formats. When in "Clock, Language and Region", choosing "Region" and clicking on "Formats" then on "Additional Settings" the user is able to change the format of numbers, especially the decimal separator, the currency and the date format, especially the English (month-day) and European (day-month) formats. Moreover, it is always a good idea to check that the list separator be set always to semicolon. Otherwise, Excel's functions will not work properly.

2.2.1. Keyboards and languages

Before starting this section, it is necessary to take a close look at your keyboard. Locate these keys since they will be used in the rest of this manual and are very useful in many programs:

English keyboard	German keyboard	Italian Keyboard	Main function
CTRL	STRG	CTRL	
Windows	Windows	Windows	Activate shortcuts in Windows 8
ALT	ALT	ALT	
ALTGR	ALTGR	ALTGR	Produce character on the key's right left
F1 to F12	F1 to F12	F1 to F12	
DEL	ENTF	CANC	Delete next character
INS	EINFG	INS	Toggle insert/overwrite mode
HOME or ▯	POS1	▯	Go to beginning
END	ENDE	FINE	Go to end
PG▯ and PG▯	BILD▯ and BILD▯	PAG▯ and PAG▯	Go one page up or down
BACKSPACE or ←	←	←	Delete last character
ENTER or ↵	↵	INVIO or ↵	Enter data
TAB or ▯	▯	TAB or ▯	Move through the window
SHIFT or ⇧	⇧	⇧	Capitalize letters
CAPS LOCK or ⇩	⇩	⇩	Keep SHIFT pressed
ARROWS ▯ ▯ ▯ ▯	▯ ▯ ▯ ▯	▯ ▯ ▯ ▯	Move the cursor

In this book, the English name for keys will be indicated. When A+B is indicated, it means that the user must press key A, then press key B, and then release both keys.

Another operation which can be useful in a multilanguage environment is changing the keyboard. While this can be done from the Language menu of the Control Panel, it is much easier to adjust it directly from the right side of the application bar, simply clicking on keyboard icon and selecting the appropriate one. If no keyboard's choice appears on the application bar, just press SHIFT with the left ALT key to toggle among available keyboard's settings.

2.3. File system

Before starting this section, it is necessary to do the following operations:

1. Press Windows+I
2. open the Control Panel
3. choose "Appearance and Personalization"
4. choose "Folder Options"
5. choose "View."
6. deselect "Hide extensions for known file types."

In this way extensions (see section 2.3.3) are shown and file types are better recognized.

2.3.1. Files and directories

Software is stored on storage devices in a special container called <u>file</u>. The operating system uses a lot of files for itself and for its data, a program usually uses one file for itself and other files for its data, and the user uses some files for his data. A file is represented by a small picture called icon.

Another special object is the <u>directory</u> or <u>folder</u>, which is basically a container for files and other directories and is represented with an icon depicting a yellow closed or open folder. Double-clicking on a directory opens a new window which presents the directory content.

Each storage device is a big directory, accessible from My Computer window, which contains directories and files. Each of these subdirectories may contain other files and other sub-subdirectories, and so on in a <u>hierarchical</u> way, forming a <u>tree</u> with the hard disk (or another storage device) as the root, directories as branches and files as leaves. On UNIBZ computers, the usual hard disk are "C:" which contains programs, "E:" which contains courses information and "F:" which contains user's reserved space. Disks directories "A:" and "B:" are usually reserved for floppy disks, and "D:" or "Z:" for CD-reader.

Choosing the "View" menu of a directory windows provides the user with several different ways to look at files and directories, the most important way being the Details which can show interesting information on files and directories such as their size and date of last modification.

Each file and directory can be univocally identified by its <u>absolute path</u> or <u>address</u>. For directories, it is the path which appears on the address bar of the directory window, while for files it is the path of their containing directory followed by "\" and the file name. For example, the absolute path of directory "Common" in "HP" directory in "Program Files" directory in the C: hard disk is "C:\Program Files\HP\Common" as can be seen from the address bar. While the HPeDiag.dll file has the absolute path "C:\Program Files\HP\Common\ HPeDiag.dll."

Note that, for Windows operating system, capital or small caps letters in paths are perfectly equal.

A special and tricky object is the <u>link</u> or <u>shortcut</u>. Although its icon looks like a file icon, the small curved arrow on the left corner clearly indicates that this object is a link. A link is simply an address to a file or directory; it is not a real file or directory. When the user clicks on the link, the computer behaves exactly as if the user is clicking on the real file or directory (if Windows can find the real one, which is not the case if in the meantime somebody deleted or moved it). However, any copy/move operation on the link will simply copy/move the link and not the real file or directory; especially copying/moving the link to another disk will probably cause it to malfunction. Therefore it is a good idea for novice users to avoid using links at all.

aaa.dll   aaa.dll - Shortcut

2.3.2. Files' operations

When double-clicking on a file, Windows usually starts a program. The user is often unaware of an important difference:

➢ double-clicking on a program <u>runs the program</u> which was double clicked
➢ double-clicking on a file calls the program associated with that file and runs it, at the same time telling the program to <u>open the file</u>. If no program is associated with that file type, Windows asks the user which program should open the file.

Copying a file means reproducing it to another location or to the same location with a different name. Copying a directory means reproducing it to another location, or to the same location with a different name, together with its entire tree of subdirectories and files. To <u>copy</u> a file or directory, Windows offers several methods, the most used being:

- drag the object to the destination. If a plus symbol does not appear, press CTRL key to have it appear while dragging. Release the object in the destination;
- select the object and click the right mouse button. Select "copy." Point the mouse to the destination and click the right mouse button. Select "paste." If the destination is the original location, the file name changes to "copy of …";
- select the object and press CTRL+C. Point the mouse to the destination and press CTRL+V. If the destination is the original location, the file name changes to "copy of …".

Moving a file means moving it to another location losing the file in the original place. Moving a directory means moving it to another location together with its entire tree of subdirectories and files. To <u>move</u> a file or directory windows offers several methods, the most used being:

- drag the object to the destination. If a plus or a link symbol does appear, press CTRL or SHIFT key to remove it. Release the object in the destination;
- select the object and click the right mouse button. Select "cut" and the icon becomes lighter. Point the mouse to the destination and click the right mouse button. Select "paste";

- select the object and press CTRL+X, and the icon becomes lighter. Point the mouse to the destination and press CTRL+V.

To <u>create a link</u> to a file or directory:

- drag the object to the destination of the link. If a link symbol does not appear, press CTRL+SHIFT until it appears. Release the object in the destination;
- select the object and click the right mouse button. Select "create shortcut." A link is created in the same directory.

Deleting a file means often putting it into the trash can where it can be recuperated unless the trash can is emptied. Deleting a directory means putting it to the trash can together with its entire tree of subdirectories and files. Pay special attention, since not always the trash can work as the user expects and sometimes files are deleted without passing through the trash can. To <u>delete</u> a file or directory windows offers several methods, the most used being:

- drag the object to the trash can and release it;
- select the object and click the right mouse button. Select "delete";

- select the object and press DEL key.

To rename a file or directory, simply select the object, click on the name and retype it. Usually, Windows accepts most names, but novice users should stick with only letters, numbers, and spaces, since other characters may be forbidden.

To create a new directory, simply right click the mouse and choose "New" and "Folder." After the creation, rename it.

 Sometimes files occupy a lot of space and need to be reduced to save disk space or to be sent by email; other times files must be put in a package to remain together or to be sent as a single file via email. These two operations are accomplished by compressing a set of files and directories,

which means using a special program (WinZip or 7-Zip or IZArc or the operating system itself) to reduce (from 0% to 90% depending on the file type) the file size and produce a new single file called zip-archive containing all the selected files and directories.

To compress a set of files and directories:

1. select the files and directories altogether,
2. click the right mouse key,
3. select "IzArc" or the installed compression program and select something like "Add to Archive File...",
4. a dialog box appears asking you to choose the zip-archive name and its destination;
5. in this dialog box you must also choose the compression method, which is strongly suggested to be ZIP to be compatible with other programs;
6. in this dialog, an encryption method (see section 4.1 on page 20) may be chosen. If your zip-archive should be opened by anybody, then choose "None": Otherwise, if you want the zip-archive to be uncompressed only by people knowing a proper password, choose any of the encryption methods, such as "AES 128 bit", and provide the password.

Other files or directories may be added later to the zip-archive simply dragging them on the zip-archive file (this is a copy and not a move operation) if it is not encrypted.

To extract files from a zip-archive file, simply click the right mouse key on the file and from the drop-down menu choose the appropriate extract option: the content will appear in the location you have chosen, together with all its directories' structure.

When double-clicking on a compressed file, if the compression program is properly installed, it will open in a window as if it were a directory. But it is not a normal directory, it is simply a window, produced by the compression program, with the list of the zip-archives content: the user should not open files from this window since it is a very unreliable way to modify files! Files can be copied from this window to a real directory simply dragging them to the directory. When the entire content of the zip-archive has to be extracted or when the user wants to preserve the original tree structure, it is better to use the Extract button of this special window.

2.3.3. File types

Windows identifies a file type by its extension, which is everything after the last dot in the filename. Usually, it is a 3 or 4 character acronym. Using the file extension, Windows knows the file type and decides which program will open that file. If the file extension does not show up, follow the instructions at section 2.3 on page 8. The most important file types are:

File type	Typical programs that open it	Typical extensions	Typical icons
Program	itself	.exe .com .bat	
Compressed	WinZip / 7-Zip / IZArc	.zip	
Text	Notepad	.txt	
Document	Word / Acrobat / PowerPoint	.docx .doc .rtf .pdf .ppt	
Sheet	Excel	.xlsx .xls .csv	
Image	Explorer / Picture Fax Viewer / Paint / Office Picture Manager	.jpg .jpeg .gif .bmp .png	
Video	Media Player	.avi .mov .mpg .mpeg	
Audio	Media Player / WinAmp	.mp3 .wav	
Web page	Explorer	.html .htm	

2.3.4. File permissions

For each file Windows 7 operating system uses <u>permission</u>. Click the right button of the mouse on a file or directory and select "Proprieties" and "Security." The security dialog box shows the list of users or groups of users who may access this object, while not listed users may not access it. For each user or group this dialog box displays the permissions, the most important being:

- <u>read</u> permission, to copy and open the object;
- <u>read and execute</u>, same as read, plus run the object if it is a program;
- <u>list content</u> (for directories), to see the content;
- <u>write</u> permission (for directories), to create files and subdirectories;
- <u>modify</u> permission (also called, when referred to a file, write permission), same as read and execute, plus delete, move, rename, save modifications;
- <u>full control</u>, same as modify, plus change permissions.

The owner of the file usually has full control over it and may change permissions or add new authorized groups or users. A special group is the Administrators group (containing the users involved in the technical administration of computers) which has full control over every object.

2.3.5. Network folders at UNIBZ

On UNIBZ LAN there are shared hard disks on which common information is stored so that it is accessible from every computer. These are called <u>network folders</u>. Some of them are:

- \\ubz01fst\courses\course_coletti which contains utility files that will be used during the course. These files must never be opened double-clicking from here. Otherwise, they will be locked (see section 2.3.4 on page 12); they should be copied on each user's desktop before opening them;
- \\ubz01fst\courses\exam_coletti\, followed by user's login name or the user's last name and first name, which will contain exam files and which is accessible only by the user;
- \\ubz01fst\students\, followed by year, faculty and user's login name, contains a copy of the student's disk F, desktop, and configuration.

2.3.6. Roaming user profile at UNIBZ

Whenever the user logs in on a new computer, usually he should find a completely new profile (Desktop, icons, Documents, configuration), which is obviously very annoying. In order to let him find always his stuff as it has been left on the last computer used, whenever the user logs off all his profile is copied on the directory

\\ubz01fst\students\, followed by year, faculty and user's login name (for example, for Diana Pfeifer enrolled in 2012 it is \\ubz01fst\students\User2012\Eco\dpfeifer). Whenever he logs in again on any university's computer, that computer retrieves all his profile's stuff from this directory.

This mechanism, called roaming user profile, works fine only if the user is not using too much disk space (which is usually 300 MB, but it is a good idea to stay below 150 MB). If the user is over quota, the system sends a warning via email to the user and, if the user remains over quota, this mechanism does not work anymore. Moreover, if the user still remains over quota, he will be forbidden from saving any file on the computer he is currently using.

Therefore it is a good idea to always work on a USB pen drive (which is then copied on another personal computer) and to periodically check the disk space looking at the proprieties of this directory. If a warning email has been received or, even worse, roaming user profile does not work anymore, files need to be deleted not from the current computer (since the mechanism is not working anymore) but directly going through this directory.

3. COMPUTER NETWORKS

This part of the book is dedicated to computer networks from a user's perspective. Nowadays a computer is very likely to belong to some company's network, or to be connected to the Internet via an Internet provider, and is therefore exposed to all the typical network problems. Without entering into technical details, this section will explore the situations in which a novice user can find himself in troubles and how he can try to survive to dialogue with network administrators in their own strange technical language.

3.1. Technical aspects

A computer network is a set of devices which communicate and share resources. These devices are mostly computers, and sometimes stand-alone hard disks, telephones, printers, and terminals (processorless computers which must rely on other computers to work).

3.1.1. Server and client

A computer network interaction is based on the client-server architecture. When considering a single interaction, one computer is the server, and the other one is the client. The server is the computer which is offering its resource, usually programmed to wait until someone asks for its resource. The client is the computer which uses the resource, which sends the request to a waiting server.

For example, when sending a document to the printer, the user's computer is the client while the printer is the server; when retrieving personal emails, the user's computer is the client which connects to the mail server asking for available emails. When talking to a friend on an Internet chat, the interaction is composed of two different interactions: the user's computer as a client is connected to the chat room's computer acting as a server, and the friend's computer does the same interaction.

The same computer may be the client for a service and the server for another service. For example, a library computer may have a CD inside its reader shared to the network (server for the CD) and may be at the same time used by a user to print his own documents (client for the printer).

3.1.2. Areas

Computer networks are commonly divided into three categories:

- Local Area Network (LAN or Intranet), usually the network of computers in the same building or belonging to the same owner. Inside the LAN every computer is well identified and usually every user is known. It is considered a trusted area.
- Wide Area Network (WAN or Internet), which is everything which connects LANs. Computers' and users' identification is very hard, and anonymity is possible. It is considered a dangerous area.
- Virtual Private Network (VPN) is a way to recognize a computer outside the LAN as a trusted computer: the user is identified with a password and his computer, even though connected via the Internet, will be considered as part of the LAN, for as long as it remains connected. VPN is typically required to identify portable computers connected via wireless connection.

3.1.3. Transfer speed

The network connecting components are the cables, which determine the speed of the LAN. Cables have a speed measured in bps (bits per second) which indicates how many bits can flow through the cable in one second.

- Ethernet cables have a speed of 10 Mbps and can thus carry 1.25 MB each second, meaning that, for example, a 600 MB movie can be transferred in 8 minutes from one computer to another one, supposing no one (neither users nor computers) is using that network tract for other purposes during the transfer.
- Fast Ethernet cables have a speed of 100 Mbps.
- Gigabit Ethernet cables have a speed of 1 Gbps.
- A wireless network, a cableless network where computers use radio signals to communicate, has usually a speed around 30-80 Mbps, depending on the wireless generation.

To find out how much time does it take to transfer a file with a size expressed in bytes, divide the connection speed in bps by 8 to find out the byte rate per second and then divide the file size by the speed to find out the number of seconds it takes for the file transfer. For example, to transfer a 600 MB file through a Fast Ethernet connection, find out the speed of 12.5 MB per second (12,500,000 bytes per second) and then divide 600 MB (or 600,000,000 bytes) by 12.5 (or by 12,500,000) to find out the time of 48 seconds.

3.2. Communication

Inside a computer network, many communication programs are installed on Intranet computers to connect to the Internet or even to internal computers.

3.2.1. Web browser

A web browser is a client program to navigate the WWW and retrieve web pages. It runs directly on the user's computer as a client and connects to external web-servers, identified with the www prefix in the Internet name, to retrieve web pages. The market leader with about 60% (www.w3schools.com, November 2014) is the browser from Google Chrome, followed by Mozilla Firefox, an open source software with 23%, Microsoft Internet Explorer, a freeware proprietary software with 10% and Safari, the browser for Mac OS X,

3.2.2. Mail reader

A mail reader is a client program to send and retrieve emails. It runs directly on the user's computer as a client and connects to a mail server, a program in charge of collecting and dispatching emails. The market leader is Microsoft Outlook, a commercial proprietary software. It has many competitors, the most famous being the open source Mozilla Thunderbird and the free Windows Live Mail.

Another way to read and send emails is through webmail systems, which are websites where the user can enter and read his received email and send new ones acting directly on the mail-server, without downloading them nor using any client. It can be useful for various reasons: it does not require the installation of a mail reader program; old received emails are always available on the website and can thus be accessed from home, office and while traveling, even without a personal laptop; the mail server takes care of emails backup. But on the other hand, it requires a continuous fast connection even to write a single long email, which can be costly and, in some situations, impossible and usually the email space is limited. The most famous website interfaces are the Microsoft Outlook Web App, where the web interface looks exactly like Microsoft Outlook, and the Webmail interface, used and personalized by most Internet providers.

3.2.3. Posta Elettronica Certificata PEC

When sending an email, the sender has no proof that it has been sent, for example, to be used in a court of justice, and no guarantee that the email has been dispatched. Some mail readers use a receipt system, but the receiver is not obliged to send back the receipt.

In order to overcome these problems, many solutions have been proposed. The Italian Posta Elettronica Certificate (PEC) system has become one of the most widespread solutions, thanks to law Decreto Ministeriale 6 May 2009 which guarantees a free PEC email address to every citizen and thanks to law 82/2005 which determines that PEC receipts are legal proves.

When an email is sent from a PEC address to another PEC address, the sender receives two receipt: the first one is a proof that the email has been sent with date and time, while the second one is a proof that the email has been dispatched to the mailbox of the receiver (or, equivalently, received by the sender). This does not represent a proof that the email has been actually read, but from the moment the email is dispatched to the mailbox, it is the receiver's responsibility to read it. Under this circumstances, it is perfectly equivalent to "raccomandata con ricevuta di ritorno." Emails can be sent also from a PEC address to a non-PEC address, and in this case, the receiver gets only the sent proof but not the dispatched-received proof, like the "raccomandata semplice." When an email is sent from a non-PEC address to a PEC address, no receipt is produced, and this is equivalent to a standard letter.

Moreover, even though it is not officially required, PEC to PEC also guarantees that content is not altered, and that sender's email address is the indicated one. However, it is important to note that PEC alone does not guarantee that the sender is really the person who claims to be and that content remains unread until it reaches the destination. In order to overcome these last two problems, encryption and digital signature (see section 4.1 on page 20) must be used.

3.2.4. Voice over IP programs

Voice over IP (VoIP) programs is able to use the computer connection as a substitute for the standard telephone. Equipped with either microphone and headphones or with a real telephone-like device, the user can send his voice through the Internet to remote computers or even to real remote telephones, thus saving on telephone bills.

VoIP requires a subscription to a VoIP's website, the most famous being Skype, who decides the telephone fares. Typically calling other VoIP's users is free all over the world, while calling fixed telephones depends only on the destination country and is independent of the caller's country, with a fare which is comparable to the standard local telephone call (about 2 €cent/minute in February 2014). On the other hand, calling mobile telephones is, for the moment, still very expensive (about 7 €cent/minute in February 2014); for this reason, special VoIP telephones, which can be programmed to automatically decide between VoIP and the standard telephone line according to the dialed number, are appearing on the market.

A similar system is WhatsApp messaging system, in practice an "SMS over IP" system in which people exchange messages and multimedia material through a chat system installed on mobile devices. The major difference with respect to most Internet communication systems is that WhatsApp uses a fully centralized architecture, i.e., all communications pass through WhatsApp company's servers, and there is never a real direct communication between two users. However, non-technical users do not realize nor care about it and thanks to its very good usability it is quickly surpassing emails' and SMS' exchanges.

3.2.5. Search engines

A search engine is a special program running on a website which offers to the user the possibility of searching other websites for specific web pages. The user needs to connect to the search engine website and digit the keywords, or sometimes even a complete question and the website returns the list of relevant web pages.

Search engines use a <u>crawler</u> technique: they continuously go through the known web pages memorizing their content and trying to discover other web pages through the contained links. In this way, they are able to memorize most of the WWW's pages (more than 8 billion pages), even though some not linked websites can remain unknown to search engines.

The most popular search engines are <u>Google</u>, the current market leader, <u>Yahoo!</u> and <u>Bing</u>. In order to choose the order in which web pages are displayed to the user, search engines use a scoring system. The most famous one is Google's which relies on the idea that a linked page is very important and useful; therefore a web page receives a score proportional to the number of web pages which put a link to it. According to recent researches, the percentage of use of these engines are Google 83%, Yahoo 6%, and Bing 4%.

There are many tricks to speed up the web search and arrive quickly to the right result:

- most novice users search the WWW using only a single keyword, which often produces the right result but in some cases can result in long lists of wrong results, for example when looking for Java Island using simply "java." Using as many keywords as possible often avoids wrong results, even though sometimes returns no pages if too many words are used;
- putting some words between quotation marks forces the search engine to look for the exact phrase, i.e., exactly for those words in that order and with no words in between;
- in the advanced search menu often there are very good options, such as the search of pages only in a specified language or only in a specified format, for example, .doc or .pdf;

- when looking simply for some images, it is more convenient to use the specific search rather than trying to find web pages containing them.

3.3. Internet connections

There are many different ways to connect to the Internet. Some are old technology, rather slow and used right now only when no other means are available, such as the old telephone line with a speed of 56 Kbps, the ISDN system, the GPRS and EDGE mobile phone systems. Modern technologies are called broadband:

ADSL (Asymmetric Digital Subscriber Line)	telephone line modem	500 Kbps in upload 8-20 Mbps download	Speed depends on subscription fee and network traffic
Internet cable	Special contract	some Gbps	
UMTS (Universal Mobile Telecommunications System) 3G HSDPA (High-Speed Downlink Packet Access)	3G mobile phone	5 Mbps in upload 40 Mbps in download	Speed depends strongly on environment
LTE (Long Term Evolution) 4G	LTE mobile phone	up to 100 Mbps	Depends on coverage and contract
Wireless Wi-Fi	wireless card	30-300 Mbps	Speed depends on wireless generation
WiMAX	the antenna in the line of sight modem	40 Mbps	Speed depends strongly on distance

Many fast connections, especially ADSL, suffer from network <u>congestion</u>: too many users are connecting at the same time, and the Internet provider's main cables are not able to support the users' maximum speed multiplied by the number of users, and therefore must reduce the practical connection speed. Therefore the maximum speed is often only theoretical, and some providers are offering a "<u>minimum band guaranteed</u>": a minimum speed under which the connection may never fall.

Unfortunately, even in technologically advanced countries, there are still many areas where nor ADSL neither UMTS arrives, mostly due to the geographic conditions (mountains, islands or long desert distances) and to the low inhabitants' density. This phenomenon is called <u>digital divide</u>: there are people (e.g., 5,000,000 of Italian inhabitants) that even willing to pay cannot get a broadband connection, and, on the other hand, Internet services and especially the WWW is continuously going towards large size contents, cutting these people off. In order to overcome this social problem, WiMAX is spreading, a sort of very long-range Wireless which arrives up to 10 Km but works only if the transmitting and receiving antennas are in the line of sight and whose theoretical speed of 70 Mbps decreases with distances to about 40 Mbps.

4. COMPUTER SECURITY

Being connected to the Internet means giving anybody access to the computer. Despite the traditional novice user's belief that he is the one who goes outside, it is instead the Internet world which is coming inside, with all its benefits and dangers. Knowing a few security issues is nowadays necessary even to the non-expert user, to avoid being lured into traps or adopting potentially dangerous behaviors.

Moreover, the recent Italian law 196/2003 on privacy issues contains in the Allegato B the minimal security techniques which must be adopted by system administrators but also by normal users. These law requirements apply clearly to all companies and professionals which handle data, but they also apply to personal users who communicate data. To personal users who do not communicate data still the security requirements to avoid data theft apply.

Law 196/2003, in particular, splits data into:

- personal data
- sensitive data: data about race and ethnicity, religious / philosophical / political opinions, belonging to religious / philosophical / political / workers organization
- sensitive data about health and sex
- justice data, which have the same prescriptions as sensitive data
- genetic data, which need extremely particular procedures which will not be described here.

Law 196/2003 prescribes that:

- each user must be authenticated by a personal username and a password or a biometric device or a personal token;
- each user must have its own permissions, limited only to the data he needs for his work, and the permissions must be revoked when the user does not need them anymore;
- users must receive specific training or instructions to be able to use their authentication and to be aware of their responsibilities, duties and the possible dangers;
- all data must be backed up (see section 4.6 on page 30) at least every week;
- security software must be updated at least every year and or 6 months when handling sensitive data;
- sensitive data receive special care: they must be stored and transmitted using encryption or the people must be unidentifiable, for example by assigning to each person's data a numeric code instead of his name and surname.

4.1. Encryption

Encryption is a text masking technique, derived from military use, which transforms information in such a way that it may be correctly read only with a special password called key. It uses two keys, a public key for encrypting, usually known only to one computer or person, and a private key for decrypting, usually known by all the computers or people which legitimately may read the information. The size of these keys, and thus the difficulty to be guessed, is expressed in bits, with 128 bits being the type most secure size used.

The two following schemas illustrate how B, C, and D can send secret messages using A's public key.

The sent messages are encrypted and later decrypted by A with his private key. In case somebody intercepts a message, he is unable to decrypt it correctly since he does not have A's private key 🔑, which is known only to A. Even when somebody 🔒 uses the public key to decrypt, it does not work.

The same process happens whenever a browser tries to send a password or secret information to a website using a secure connection (see section 4.5 on page 29): the website tells the browser its public key, and the browser uses it to encrypt information which can be read only by the arriving website.

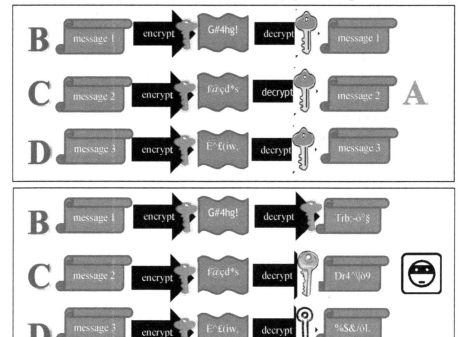

Another analogous usage of encryption is to make stored data unreadable except by the owner. In this case private and public keys coincide and are kept secret. The encryption and decryption process is done automatically by a program (PDF creation programs or compression programs can do it, see page 11 for instructions how to do it) or even by the operative system (if the entire disk is encrypted), which asks the password to the user every time.

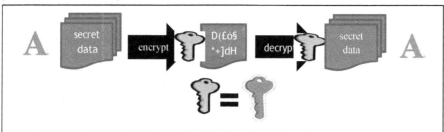

4.1.1. Digital signature

A digital signature, or electronic signature, is an encryption technique for documents which guarantees, at the same time, the document's author's identity and that the document's content has not been altered. According to Italian <u>law 82/2005</u>, the digital signature is equivalent to a handwritten signature.

The two following schemas illustrate instead the use of encryption for digital signature. A wants to publish a publicly available document with its signature. It is sufficient for A to encrypt it with his private key 🔑 and all the users can try to decrypt it with A's public key 🔑. If the result of decryption is something readable, it means that the document was really encrypted with A's private key and thus comes from A; on the other hand, if the result is unreadable, it means that encryption was not done with A's private key. In this way, digital signature used in combination with PEC can guarantee also sender's identity and email's content.

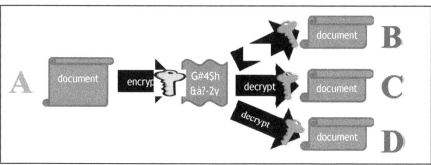

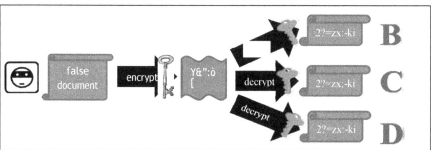

While encryption to receive secret messages or to hide information simply requires the user or the program to create its own couple of private and public keys (programs, for example, browsers, do this operation automatically without the user's intervention), for digital signature it is not so simple. Since everybody must be sure that the public key is really the author's public key, digital signature requires a <u>certification</u>

authority to distribute private and public keys. Even though theoretically a simple password is enough, to be sure that the user does not give the private password around, the certification authority gives him, after having identified him through a governmental identity card, a password usually together with another identification tool (a smart card, a telephone number for an OTP to be send), which, when used together, correspond to his private key. An automatic signature program takes care of automatically encrypting documents.

Several Italian public institutions are now using the national health care card as a smart card and, using it as certification of user's identity, offer access to many services, even though they do not offer yet the digital signature of personal documents. The service to digitally sign documents is offered by private certification companies, with prices currently affordable also by private users and with alternative devices such as smartcards or OTP devices (see section 4.2.1 on page 25).

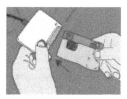

4.1.2. Keys expiration

The major drawback of encryption keys is that if a computer is put to work trying to encrypt text with

many private keys in sequence and then to decrypt it with the correct public key , within some years it will manage to find the right private key which leads to a correct encryption-decryption. Therefore, each couple of private-public keys has a time-limited duration, usually some years, after which it is necessary to change them and encrypt again all the past documents.

Documents for which it is important to determine the exact date of the signature have moreover a temporal mark signed directly by the certification authority.

4.1.3. Comparison with a handwritten signature

	Digital signature	Handwritten signature
Who can sign	Needs keys from a certification authority and proper tools	Everybody instantly
Who can verify	Everybody (with proper tools)	Handwriting analysts
Verification reliability	Sure for some years	Subjective in dubious cases, no time limit
Temporal duration	Some years (can be renewed)	Until other reliable signatures are available
Mass signatures	Some seconds for all documents (with proper tools)	Some seconds per document
Date reliability	Objective if the temporal mark	Based on other subjective elements (paper's and ink's age)

4.2. Passwords

On the Intranet the user is identified only by his username, known to everybody, and his password, known only to him. The password is what makes an unknown person an authenticated user, with all his privileges and his identity's responsibilities. If somebody else uses the right user's password, for the Intranet this other person is exactly the user. Law 196/2003 explicitly forbids users from giving their password to other users, even when they are absent from work. These are some, often underestimated, malign actions a passwords' thief can do:

- steal personal information: the thief can read the user's emails and personal information;

- steal privacy protected data: the thief can gain access to data about other people protected by privacy, or read emails received from other people. The legal responsibility of this privacy violation is the thief as well as the user who did not protect other people's data;
- steal money: the thief can find the user's bank account numbers and passwords, sometimes directly from the user's web browser's history;
- delete and modify data: the thief can delete user's important data, or even worse he can modify these data without the user's knowledge (bank numbers, friend's email addresses, degree thesis content, add illegal pictures);
- steal an identity: for the computer, the thief is now the user, and therefore he can act to the outside world exactly as if it were the user, for example answering to emails, subscribing to websites, withdrawing from exams;
- start illegal activities: anybody who wants to start an illegal Internet activity will obviously use somebody else identity, so he will not get into troubles when the activity is discovered.

Therefore it is absolutely necessary to keep passwords secret. Unfortunately, many people use very trivial passwords. This is the list of the most common passwords in 2014: password, 123456, 12345678, 1234, qwerty, dragon, pussy, baseball, football, letmein, monkey, 696969, abc123, 12345.

There exist automatic programs which are able to try 4 billion passwords each second, and they usually start trying combinations of words and numbers (the complete set of all Italian, German and English words can be tried in less than 1 second). Check on https://howsecureismypassword.net how much time does it take to one of these programs to discover your easy passwords.

Law 196/2003 explicitly requires that password does have some features:

- change the password often, at least every six months (3 if sensitive data are handled);
- avoid words related to yourself, such as names, birth dates, birthplaces, and addresses;
- use minimum 8 characters.

Moreover, other good procedures are:

- use as a password a good mix of numbers, strange characters, small caps and capital letters, avoiding any common word (other people's names or words which can be found in a dictionary);
- use different passwords for different purposes. Unfortunately, every website asks the user to register with a password and users who use always the same password are giving it away to every website they register, even untrustworthy ones. It is a good procedure to have at least three passwords: one for important use (bank account), the second one for everyday use and the last one for unimportant use (registering to unknown websites or to services that will not be used anymore).
- beware of passwords stored in programs: mail readers, Internet Explorer, and many other programs store your password masked with asterisks. They seem to be unreadable, but computer experts can reveal them instantly. Store passwords in programs only if that computer has a single user (i.e., the home computer or the personal laptop) or if access to that computer is on a username basis, but never in public places such as an Internet café.

4.2.1. Alternative password devices

Law 196/2003 gives the possibility to either replace the password authentification with other personal devices or with biometric identification or to simply add these techniques to existing passwords.

Usually, biometric identification is considered to be very secure, and thus it is used to replace completely the password system. It can be <u>fingerprint</u> recognition, <u>hand palm</u> blood vessels recognition, eye's <u>retina scanning</u> or voice <u>identification</u>.

For very important activities, such as a digital signature or bank operations, usually, a personal device is instead added to the standard login and password system. The usual password is remembered personally by the user, and a personal device provides the second part of the password. This device can be a <u>smart card</u>, such as the national health care, which is inserted into a card reader or a <u>USB token</u> and they provide to the program or website the second half of the password which is stored inside the object. Alternatively, the second part of the password is an <u>OTP</u> One Time Password, generated every time through a <u>telephone call</u> to user's mobile phone or displayed on a small <u>token</u> (which can be either inserted or not inserted in a USB plug) which is clearly synchronized with the website for which password is needed. This big advantage of this second system is that, even if both parts of the password are intercepted or guessed, the second part can be used only that time and will expire after a few seconds.

4.3. Viruses

From the Internet, many unauthorized connection attempts arrive. Some of these are mistakenly authorized and manage to reach the Intranet or at least to come in contact with programs which are behind the firewall. If these connections carry malign intentions, usually their aim is to explore and use the Intranet computers, to destroy Intranet data or to stop some Intranet services (which is a dangerous attack if these services are managing stock trades or telephone calls). Defense against these kinds of attacks is in charge system administrators.

While normal external attacks do not involve normal users, the virus is a special attack which arrives directly on the user's computer and must be prevented and stopped by him. The virus is a little program which has this name because its life cycle is the same as a biological organism: survive and duplicate.

1. It arrives on the computer through email attachments, downloaded files, CDs and floppy disks or directly from the Intranet. It is often hidden inside other good files or programs, which are called infected. In the last years, many free programs deliberately install small advertisement programs without the user's explicit consent; this kind of behaviors is considered borderline between a virus and a way of financing the program's development.

2. As soon as the user mistakenly runs it (often trying to run the good program or to open the good file), the virus orders the computer to run itself every time the computer is turned on, thus assuring its survival.

3. It starts duplicating itself, infecting other files, CDs, and floppy disks, and trying to send itself around by email or on the Intranet.

4. Most viruses are programmed to do damage to the computer and to the user, altering or deleting files, sending emails with user's personal data, preventing firewalls and antiviruses from running, or turning the computer off. No viruses are known to be able to damage hardware.

Many names are used for viruses' types according to their different behaviors.

- trojan horse is a virus which looks like a good program, and when downloaded and run by the user, it performs the user's wanted task but at the same time does other actions;
- keylogger is a virus which records keyboard's activity and then sends the keystrokes to its creator, mostly to get user's passwords;
- back door is a virus which opens a port on the computer to let external users in;
- adware is a virus which displays advertisement;
- spyware is a virus which spies user's activity to get passwords or to target the user with specific advertisement;
- ransomware is a virus which makes its presence public and demands to the user money to be removed, threatening to damage him in a variety of ways, such as encrypting files or pretending to be an authority's tool and asking the payment of a fine, as the famous Italian "Polizia di stato" virus does.

These types are not exclusive: for example, a Trojan horse which is at the same time a spyware and an adware.

An infected computer can be recognized by some symptoms. These are the most frequent ones:

- when the computer is turned on, unwanted programs start, advertisement appears, and the desktop presents some new bars or features which were not present nor installed before;
- the computer starts very slowly, and unknown programs give strange operating system errors;
- commercial or pornographic web pages appear on the web browser without the user's consent;

- the analogical modem makes typical connection noises even when the computer is not connected, or the operating system asks the user to stop the current connection and start a new one to a strange telephone number;
- the Task Manager window (see page 7) presents unknown programs.

Most of the time, a responsible user's behavior it the best weapon against viruses: it protects him from getting viruses, helps him removing them and prevents him from diffusing them. Responsible behavior means:

- never open downloaded files and email attachments, especially when they come from a friend with a text such as "please open it, urgent!", since simulating to be a user's friend is a typical virus tactic. To open these files, save them on the desktop, check them with antivirus and then open them;
- do not insert in your computer CDs, DVDs and USB pen drives coming from other people or which were inserted in other computers, unless you have an antivirus running or unless you scan them immediately with an antivirus;
- avoid visiting strange websites, especially pornographic or hackers' website, or websites which open a lot of pop-up windows;
- have an antivirus always running or at least run an updated antivirus on your whole hard disks every week (while Italian law currently prescribes minimum every 6 months); keep your antivirus always up to date: more than 50 new viruses appear every week;
- keep communication programs and Microsoft products up to date. Microsoft and most software companies offer free updates and automatic updating tools;
- beware of free programs which often try to install adware programs, asking the permission very quickly during installation's steps, relying on the novice user's habit of clicking always "yes."

To check the computer for viruses and to try to remove viruses from the computer, the user can run a special program called antivirus. The antivirus basically has three possible different actions:

- ➢ it can scan all the storage devices (hard disks, the floppy disk inside the computer, the CD or DVD inside the reader) for viruses. If a virus is found, it tries to remove it and to repair damaged files. Some files can be unrecoverable. Complete devices scanning takes usually some hours;
- ➢ it can scan a single file or an entire directory for viruses. If there is an infected file, it tries to delete the virus and repair it. Some files can be unrecoverable. Single file scanning takes some seconds;
- ➢ it can be always running. In this case, whenever a virus or a suspect file is run, the antivirus prevents it from running and warns the user.

A lot of antivirus programs, free and commercial, exist. Their most important feature is obviously the possibility to be constantly updated through the Internet.

4.4. Emails

4.4.1. Attachments

For viruses, email attachments are a first-class way of traveling, since they are very often opened by users without any precaution. Sometimes viruses hide inside files which were really sent by the sender, unaware of having an infected computer. Other times a virus takes control of the mail reader program and sends itself to the whole address book, counterfeiting the sender address (often using an address taken from the address book) in order to avoid that the real infected computer be identified and to gain the thrust of the receiver, and writing in the email text smart sentences pretending to be a regular friend of the receiver. The arrival of this kind of email usually creates havoc, since the receiver is sure that the fake sender has a virus, while the original infected computer is another one.

The basic rule is never open any attachment from the mail reader program. <u>Save</u> the attached files on the desktop and <u>run</u> an antivirus program to check these files before <u>opening</u> them. Even when the email comes from a friend: he cannot know that to have got a virus, or he can not be the real sender.

4.4.2. Spam

<u>Spam</u> messages are <u>unsolicited, unwanted bulk</u> emails. They are unsolicited, meaning that the user did not ask to receive them, they are unwanted, meaning that the user did not want to receive them, and they are bulk, meaning that they are sent to millions of addresses. They are used mainly for four different purposes:

- <u>advertisement</u> emails are the most innocuous version. The email message contains commercial information usually on medicines, pornography, software or investments. Sometimes these messages are purposely written with orthographic mistakes or with strange characters, to avoid being intercepted by antispam programs;

- <u>chain letters</u> are electronic versions of letters circulating in the XX century. They promise good luck to anyone resending it and bad luck to anyone trashing it, or they contain a sad story of an ill child desiring postcards or an urgent warning about a terrible virus: their content is probably false or too old, and a search on the WWW will reveal this immediately. Sending it around will probably cause complains from other users;

- <u>frauds</u> are usually long letters proposing the user semi-legal bargain or a big lottery prize. Their only aims are to get the user's bank coordinates for further illicit activities and to lure him into paying small expenses hoping to get the promised imaginary money;

- phishing emails look as completely plausible emails from banks, credit card companies or website which handle money, asking the user to enter their website to perform some urgent actions. They often carry real logos, seem to address to the correct website and even cite the real website's anti-phishing campaign! However, this website address is a trap, and the user will be sent to a false website, who looks exactly like the original one, whose only scope is to get passwords or credit card numbers. Phishing has become a big problem for Internet banking system, and the user's best defenses are entering any crucial website always typing the address directly in the web browser (never clicking on addresses contained in emails) and calling immediately his own bank at the telephone whenever believing of having been a victim of phishing.

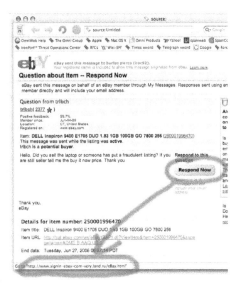

The best behavior to adopt against spam messages is to ignore them. Complaining is worthless since their sender address is always false; clicking on their links, especially if they suggest to click there to be removed from their lists, usually has the only effect of letting the spammer know that the user's address is really read by someone.

The best ways to defend from spammers are to avoid using the user's main email address during registration in forums, newsgroups, and unnecessary websites, and to avoid publishing it on the personal or the company's website. These are the places where spammers get their millions of addresses. If it is really necessary, a good strategy is to have an alternative email address for registrations, which will receive all the spam.

There are antispam programs, which put the supposed spam messages in a separate junk email folder, but they are not completely reliable, and sometimes they trash even good messages. These programs rely on analysis of the email's content and on blacklists, which contains the Internet mail servers which are supposed to let spammers send their emails; it may happen that a good mail server ends up into those blacklists and that emails send from customers or employees of that Internet site are marked as spam by other sites.

4.5. Navigation

Navigation is the second most dangerous Internet activity. It has more or less the same dangers as emails: the user's computer can get viruses if he does not run an antivirus before opening downloaded files, and the user can be lured into phishing websites if he does not type personally the bank's address in the web browser. Moreover, the computer can get viruses even when simply visiting some websites, and therefore two good suggestions are to avoid visiting strange (pornographic websites, websites with a lot of pop-up windows and illegal websites) or untrustworthy websites and to keep Internet Explorer and Windows operating system always up to date.

The other security problem while navigating is <u>data interception</u>. When connecting to a website, the user's data travels long distances, passing through a large number of computers (to connect from unibz.it to www.athesia.it the data go to Padua, Milan and Bologna passing through at least 13 computers). Data on the Internet travel without any protection, any computer administrator can read them. Therefore, when sending passwords and other private data to a website, the user should take special care that the address in the address bar starts with https:// (instead of http://) and on some browser a lock icon appears in the lower right part of the windows, while on others the address bar becomes green with a lock: these indications mean that the connection is <u>secure</u> (<u>SSL</u>) since data are traveling encrypted. Beware that the SSL connection guarantees only that data is not intercepted and that the user is connected to the same website from which he started the connection, while it does not guarantee this website is the right one.

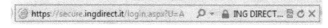

4.6. Attacks from outside

Any computer attached to the Internet, either directly through a modem or indirectly inside a LAN, is subject to attacks from the outside WAN. The typical attack consists in external computers trying to gain access to the computer using an operating system known as problems or hoping that the user is currently running programs which open some computer's parts to outside connections. From the user's side, the best defense is keeping the computer's program always up-to-date, especially the operating system and communication programs (as suggested in section 4.5 on page 29).

The most famous attack from outside and the one from which it is very difficult to have an appropriate defense is the DoS <u>Denial of Service</u> attack. It is an attack which does not strike private users, but companies offering services over the Internet. It consists in sending millions of incoming connections which pretend to use the service but stay simply connected, in such a way to overcrowd the server and drain all its resources (bandwidth, speed, memory) until the server crashes. The attacker clearly does not use his own computer to carry on a DoS attack. Otherwise, his computer would probably crash before the server but uses a computer of unaware users around the world, called zombies, which have been hacked in the past days. In this way, the attacker has the power of several dozen computers connected from many different parts of the world, and at the same time, it is difficult to trace the responsibility up to him.

4.6.1. Firewall

Often programs' security breaches once discovered need some days to be fixed and somebody can take benefit of them in this short time before the security update is installed on the user's computer. Therefore on every LAN, usually at the point where the LAN connects to the Internet, or more often on every computer a special program called firewall is running. The firewall examines all the incoming and outgoing traffic, using the following analysis techniques:

- which internal program is originating/receiving the traffic,
- from/to which external address is the traffic originated/directed,
- what amount of traffic is passing from/to the same program to/from the same external address,
- which kind of data are passing.

Making an analysis of these data clearly slows down the connection but lets the firewall stop potential unauthorized connection, putting them in a wait state until the users give his approval or denial.

Windows Seven operating system comes with a firewall preinstalled, which lets the user customize which kind of programs are allowed to make or receive connections and determine rules to approve or deny automatically connections.

4.7. Backup

Backup is the process of copying important data to another location to prevent their loss. Sometimes programs and even entire operating systems are copied, to be able to immediately continue working even when a computer breaks. There are three very good reasons to do regular backups:

- against the user, who can accidentally delete some files or who can modify files and then change his mind. Having a recent backup handy can often save hours of work;
- against the system, which can suddenly break due to hardware or software problems. Even hard disks tend to be unreliable after some years of continuous activity. A recent backup saves the user from redoing all the work of the previous months;
- against viruses and other users, which can delete and alter files: a backup can save a user coming back from vacations.

Usually, the operating system's and the programs' backup are done by system administrators: law 196/2003 explicitly requires an instantaneous backup for all sensitive data, and that data is restored within 7 days in case of loss. However, there are some files which should be taken in charge by the user himself:

- personally created data files, including all documents and images created by the user, and any other file which is a result of the user's personal work;
- in case emails are not handled with an online system: the contacts, calendar and the emails (mail readers usually offer a way to save them into files to be used for backup);
- some programs require a lot of configuration and store their configuration in configuration files, which are usually in the program's directory;
- all the stuff which is difficult to find again, such as documents from other people or downloaded from forgotten websites.

The place where the files are copied determines the reliability of the backup. It should be a large, cheap and fast storage device. It should also be handy, since the typical problem with backup is that the user does not take time to do it regularly and, when the backup is too old, it is worthless. For home or simple office users, the Friday morning backup is a good timing solution. Good storage devices to be used are:

- a second hard disk, used only for backup, which is very fast and very large and always ready to be used;

- online backup systems, where user's data are uploaded and are ready from anywhere in the world (given a broadband connection), with Dropbox, Google Drive, Box and Amazon Cloud being the most famous and offering some GB of space for free;

- <u>USB pen drive</u>, to be used only in an emergency when no other appropriate storage device is available;
- big companies usually have special <u>tape devices</u> for backups.

4.7.1. RAID

A very popular backup solution is <u>RAID</u> (Redundant Array of Independent Disks) technology, which consists of several identical hard disks. There are different types of RAID implementations, which vary a lot in functionalities and security.

<u>JBOD</u> (Just a Bunch Of Disks) is a primitive form of the RAID in which all the disks are seen by the user simply as disks on which they can write as usual. The advantage is that the available space is the sum of the space of all the disks. However there is no form of data protection: if a disk breaks, anything on that disk is lost.

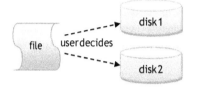

<u>RAID0</u> uses two identical disks which are seen by the user as a single disk. Every time he writes a file, the first part of the file is written on the first disk while the second on the second this. This strategy has the big advantage that is writing speed doubles, with a total available space which is the sum of the size of the two disks. But if a disk breaks, all the content of both disks is lost, since the user will lose half of all the files.

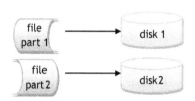

<u>RAID1</u> is the most common implementation of the RAID. It uses two identical disks, but the user sees only the first one. The second disk is simply an identical and instantaneous copy of the first one. The disadvantage is that the speed does not improve, and the available space is the size of one disk only, but in case of a disk breaks, no file is lost since the other one is its identical copy. This is a very good backup solution to protect data against physical failure, especially suited for 24h services. However, it is not a backup solution against viruses or user's incidental cancellations, since any modification on the first disk is immediately performed on the second one.

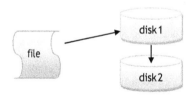

RAID10 is an overlay of RAID1 and RAID0. It uses four disks, writing files on the first and on the third as if they were on RAID0 and then duplicating their content on disks two and four. This technique has the speed of RAID0, the reliability of RAID1, but gives the user a space equivalent to the sum of two disks sizes, while four disks are effectively used.

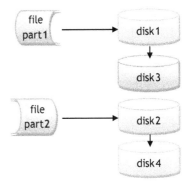

All the RAID techniques are good at either improving the speed or improving the reliability against hardware failure, but are not good against other threats and therefore they must always be coupled with another form of back-ups, such as tape backup for large companies or weekly/daily copy on DVD or on another hard disk for home users.

www.ingramcontent.com/pod-product-compliance
Lightning Source LLC
Chambersburg PA
CBHW070904070326
40690CB00009B/1993